If You Give a Mommy a Glass of Wine

by Renee Charytan

Illustrated by Rick Van Hattum

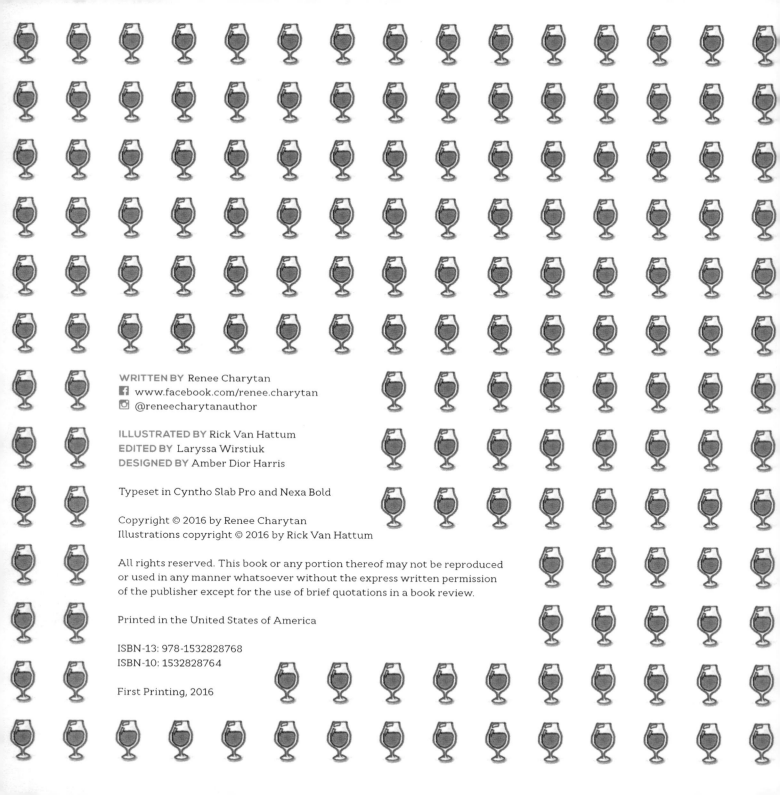

WRITTEN BY Renee Charytan
 www.facebook.com/renee.charytan
 @reneecharytanauthor

ILLUSTRATED BY Rick Van Hattum
EDITED BY Laryssa Wirstiuk
DESIGNED BY Amber Dior Harris

Typeset in Cyntho Slab Pro and Nexa Bold

Printed in the United States of America

ISBN-13: 978-1532828768
ISBN-10: 1532828764

First Printing, 2016

For all the imperfect mommies who work hard, try hard, and make mistakes.

In loving memory of my mother who always believed in me and encouraged me to follow my dreams.

To Ariel, Ayla, Harry, and Eve. You are my everything.

Special thanks to Amber, Jess, Jessica, Jodi, Kara, Laryssa, Rick, and Sybil.

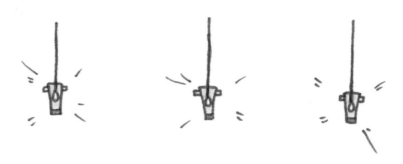

If you give a mommy a glass of wine,

she'll want the bottle.

Looking at the bottle will remind her to pack school lunches.

But packing lunches
will kill a buzz.

So she'll set a reminder
to make them tomorrow.

Then she'll want to
binge-watch her favorite show.

She may even finish the entire season!

When she notices the time,
she'll probably want to go to bed.

She may forget
to wash her face
or change out
of her clothes.

When the alarm goes off
she'll probably wish she were still sleeping.

She'll need coffee: strong and black.

She'll lose her keys and phone.

The kids will probably be late for school,

and she may end up driving
in yesterday's clothes.

On her way back, she may get carried away

and order
a triple shot of espresso.

When she's finished,
she'll have *tons* of energy!

Back home, she'll

do the laundry,

pay the bills,

check her email,

and try to organize
the entire house.

Looking at the mess
may get her so flustered
that she'll probably
    shout a few bad words and
        want to pull out her hair!

After cleaning, she'll need more coffee.

She may notice
her reflection,
and want to
take a shower.

But looking at the stove
will remind her to cook dinner.

She'll make
soup
and
veggies
and
pasta
and
rice
and
meat,

which the kids will probably find disgusting.

By then, she'll need to get out of the house,
or she may go insane!

So she'll take the dog for a walk.

Outside, her dog will notice a rabbit,

and he'll get so excited that he'll want to chase it!

She'll trip and
twist her ankle.

Next she'll want to drive to urgent care,

but her car's voice recognition
will call Aunt Claire

and direct her to Irving Cares.

By then, she'll want to take a nap.

But she'll probably grab an energy drink instead.

Then it'll be time to get the kids.

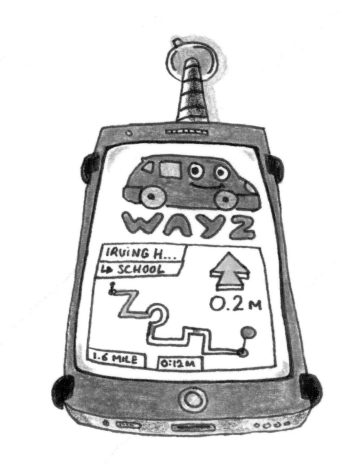

They'll climb
into the car
and
fight,
whine,
and yell
until
her head
throbs

probably
as much as her foot!

Back at home,

they'll refuse to eat,

take a bath,

do their homework,

or brush their teeth.

Finally they'll go to bed.

And eventually
they'll fall asleep.

Which means,
it'll be time for her husband to come home.

He'll ask about his dinner.

She'll glare at him, then ask for a glass of wine,

and chances are,
        she'll want a shot of whiskey to go with it.

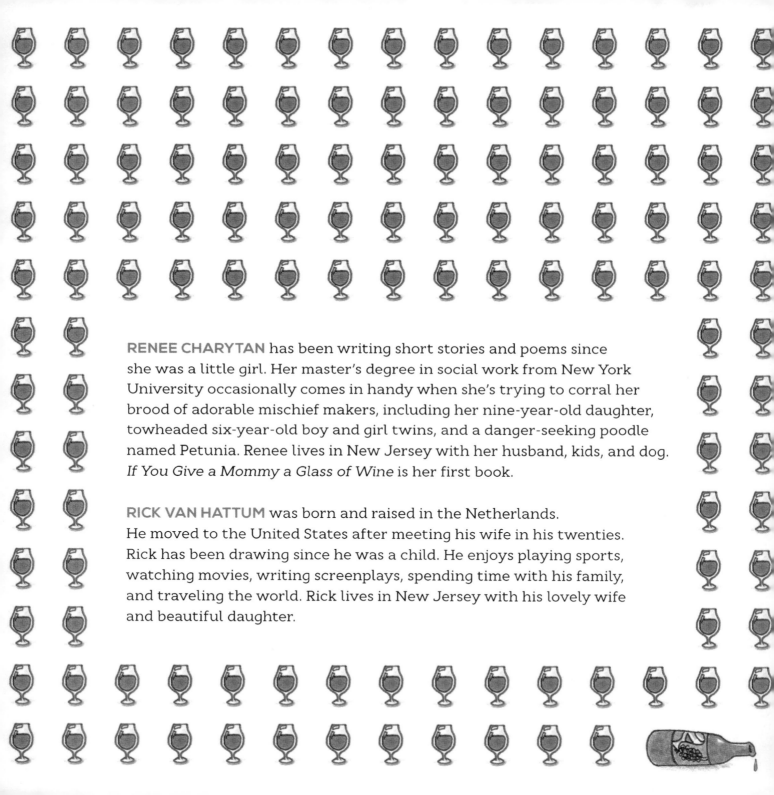

RENEE CHARYTAN has been writing short stories and poems since she was a little girl. Her master's degree in social work from New York University occasionally comes in handy when she's trying to corral her brood of adorable mischief makers, including her nine-year-old daughter, towheaded six-year-old boy and girl twins, and a danger-seeking poodle named Petunia. Renee lives in New Jersey with her husband, kids, and dog. *If You Give a Mommy a Glass of Wine* is her first book.

RICK VAN HATTUM was born and raised in the Netherlands. He moved to the United States after meeting his wife in his twenties. Rick has been drawing since he was a child. He enjoys playing sports, watching movies, writing screenplays, spending time with his family, and traveling the world. Rick lives in New Jersey with his lovely wife and beautiful daughter.

55789728R00024

Made in the USA
Lexington, KY
02 October 2016